Cub Quiz

by Nicholas Spencer

(l)Chris Wallace/Alamy; (r)Aditya Singh/age fotostock

(t)Critterbiz/Shutterstock.com; (b)Life on White/Photodisc/Getty Images

I see little eyes.

I see little ears.

(l)Chris Wallace/Alamy; (r)Aditya Singh/age fotostock

I see little teeth.

I see little noses.

(l)John E Marriott/All Canada Photos/Getty Images; (r)Roland Weihrauch/Photoshot

I see little tails.

I see little paws.

I see little cubs.

My Class

by Juan Martinez

Ken Cavanagh/McGraw-Hill Education

Ken Cavanagh/McGraw-Hill Education

I see a pencil.

Informational Text
My Little ABCs
illustrated by Steve Mack
a
b
c
Mc Graw Hill Education

I see a book.

Ken Cavanagh/McGraw-Hill Education

I see a boy.

Ken Cavanagh/McGraw-Hill Education

I see a girl.

Marko Poplasen/Shutterstock.com

I see a table.

Fancy/SuperStock

I see a teacher.

Ariel Skelley/Blend Images LLC

I see my class.